Spoken among the Trees

Poems

Jeff Gundy

The University of Akron Press
Akron, Ohio

 First Edition 2007 Manufactured in the United States of America. All inquiries and permission requests should be addressed to the Publisher, The University of Akron Press, Akron, Ohio 44325-1703.

11 10 09 08 07 5 4 3 2 1

LIBRARY OF CONGRESS CATALOGING-IN-PUBLICATION DATA
Gundy, Jeffrey Gene, 1952–
Spoken among the trees : poems / Jeff Gundy.
p. cm. — (Akron series in poetry)
Includes bibliographical references and index.
ISBN 978-1-931968-50-8 (pbk. : alk. paper)
I. Title.
PS3557.U484S66 2007
811'.54—DC22
2007043794

The paper used in this publication meets the minimum requirements of American National Standard for Information Sciences—Permanence of Paper for Printed Library Materials, ANSI Z39.48–1984. ∞

Cover image: Charles Ephraim Burchfield, *Landscape with Trees and Dandelions* (1959), watercolor on paper, 43.5" x 26.5". Mint Museum of Art, Charlotte, North Carolina. Gift of the Mint Museum Auxiliary. 1981.45

Spoken among the Trees

Akron Series in Poetry

Akron Series in Poetry

Elton Glaser, Editor

Barry Seiler, *The Waters of Forgetting*
Raeburn Miller, *The Comma After Love: Selected Poems of Raeburn Miller*
William Greenway, *How the Dead Bury the Dead*
Jon Davis, *Scrimmage of Appetite*
Anita Feng, *Internal Strategies*
Susan Yuzna, *Her Slender Dress*
Raeburn Miller, *The Collected Poems of Raeburn Miller*
Clare Rossini, *Winter Morning with Crow*
Barry Seiler, *Black Leaf*
William Greenway, *Simmer Dim*
Jeanne E. Clark, *Ohio Blue Tips*
Beckian Fritz Goldberg, *Never Be the Horse*
Marlys West, *Notes for a Late-Blooming Martyr*
Dennis Hinrichsen, *Detail from The Garden of Earthly Delights*
Susan Yuzna, *Pale Bird, Spouting Fire*
John Minczeski, *Circle Routes*
Barry Seiler, *Frozen Falls*
Elton Glaser and William Greenway, eds., *I Have My Own Song for It: Modern Poems of Ohio*
Melody Lacina, *Private Hunger*
George Bilgere, *The Good Kiss*
William Greenway, *Ascending Order*
Roger Mitchell, *Delicate Bait*
Lynn Powell, *The Zones of Paradise*
Dennis Hinrichsen, *Cage of Water*
Sharmila Voorakkara, *Fire Wheel*
Kurt Brown, Meg Kearney, Donna Reis, Estha Weiner, eds., *Blues for Bill: A Tribute to William Matthews*
Vern Rutsala, *How We Spent Our Time*
Clare Rossini, *Lingo*
Beckian Fritz Goldberg, *The Book of Accident*
Ashley Capps, *Mistaking the Sea for Green Fields*
Roger Mitchell, *Half/Mask*
Alison Pelegrin, *Big Muddy River of Stars*
Jeff Gundy, *Spoken among the Trees*

Contents

IV.

Do your eyes seek high places, soaring, some thin sky?
You and I, we aren't birds, but water in a cup.

—Nick Lindsay, "A Wedding Song"

Damselfly

Beginnings have an irritating but essential fragility,
and one that should be taken to heart.
—Teilhard de Chardin

Consider that ant swarm on the sidewalk, like spilled brown sugar,
and the pale yellow leaves the hackberry casts free in a dry
June, pressed to the parking lot.

The gray uneven two-by-fours of the picnic table, no place to set a
cup half full or half empty.

A green grain head, waving from the corner the mower can't reach.

Elijah's cloak parting the waters, and Elisha: "Let me inherit a
double-share of your spirit." And Elijah: "Your request is a
difficult one."

And the bowl with the coiled serpent in its heart. And *This is my*
body. And the stones of the creek, surfacing with the drought.

When spoken, the secret is no longer the secret. I am not good at
secrets. The God I love speaks only in roars and whispers. The
God I love only seems to play favorites.

At nine it is already humid, and the woods are dressed in their seven
summer greens. All around me the machines are sorting and
sifting, cutting and burning.

I wait a whole minute and a black damselfly crosses the creek and
the world begins again and again.

And far away right here in town, the child wakes and rolls and stretches, not yet hungry. Wide-eyed, he waves and coos to bring the day into his blue-tinted room.

And there she is, smiling in the open door.

I

Fulks Run to Cumberland

We were almost to Lost City when my companion said,
This is beautiful, but I'm so sleepy. Sleep, I said, knowing
I had the wheel and coffee in the mug, and soon

she was traveling blind beside me. I steered on
and refused every side road no matter how winding
and inviting, I let Maggies Creek Road and Narrow Lane

and Toms Knob Approach slide on by, I grumbled
only a little at the long stoplight at the one-lane bridge.
My companion was leaned way back, dreaming

of angelhaired lovers for all I knew, breathing
so easy I thought she must be hearing the sweet shoals
of the Lost River running low along the road, whispering

for half a mile before turning away as the hills said they must.
I obeyed every last curl in the road and turned up the stereo,
hoping my companion would awaken and speak: *I've been*

dreaming, you were there, goldenhaired angels were there,
we must go back and turn at Lost City, take the Narrow Lane
into the mountains. I saw a perfect seed head shaking

in the golden evening, every puff a signal and a sign.
Don't you remember what the river said as it caressed
the gray stones? Listen . . . but my companion only turned

and rode her slumber onward, leaving all the rest
to me. *Last night I dreamed that I was dreaming,*
sang the singer. A fluted hill, a long curve. On the lake,

five geese stirred, shook out their wings, and disappeared.

Advice for Walkers

Watch your step. You could fall any minute through
the hard skin of rock, the soft skin of dirt. You could find

yourself floating to an awkward reunion with the debris
you've been trailing behind you all these years.

Watch carefully. There are some who burn so bright
even a glance will leave you whirling. Watch the ground

at your feet and the last stretchy sky. There is much
in the mucky spring that you don't want to bring home

on your shoes. No one knows where the miracle
will begin, or where the disaster will start. No one knows

the name of the beloved until it is spoken, perhaps gently
when asked how to say it, Maria, or Kaitlin, or Grace.

The earth is a mirror. The sky is a lens. The trees are an echo
of their own roots, of your own roots, your lost fathers

brooding on shades of black in the quiet caves, your mothers
counting the one breath they manage each month, praying

thank you, praying goodbye. Watch your step, not the women
who glow like stars and are just as much your business.

Consider the small brick porch where your son lost his balance
years ago, where he fell hard, dizzy with love and hunger.

When your eyes have drunk a million shots of splendor
and turned back for more, when your heart has packed

and hidden every wonder, every slender ankle, every head
of curling invitations to the wrong feast, when desire

elbows memory into the bushes and runs headlong downhill
smack into the creek, when the creek closes icy

and astonishing over you, all your clothes soaked and useless,
the last veils of your secrecy torn open like the car door

after the crash, when you clamber up dripping mud
and snowmelt and the most obstinate futility since

second grade, when you fumble at the bank, scrape knuckles
on the frozen roots, on the slabs of broken ice, oh my friend,

lift your dripping useful boot and press it to the ground,
press and push and even now the world will hold you up.

Soul Travel at the Electric Brew, Goshen, Indiana

The triple-chocolate cookie was the best part of lunch, unless
it was the blonde girl walking to her car outside or the semi
with the hog trailer thundering by in full stench. At the Brew

there's some Dylanesque bluegrassy stuff playing, and the coffee is thick
as I want it. I find the black queen and a rook on the floor
and stow them back in the box, feeling smug. For the first time all week,

I'm nearly free in this town where everybody looks familiar and strange
at the same time. Twice just today I met friends who lifted
their left hands and took my left hand. At this rate, in the next life

I could be a fork or the black queen or the last bullet in a rusty gun.
I could be a cheap but decent guitar, a condom, a hooker, a fudged
and flattened map of the world. I could be a photon screaming

silently toward Arcturus, a plaid confident blouse, a floodlight
hung high on a wall. If I could, I would live everywhere for a little while,
be the man with the silver goatee who favors my friend Ervie,

be all four of those women clucking over the wreckage of lunch,
be the clock and the wall and the pawn still lost in the couch,
the murky ink waiting to inscribe some sad dumb gospel.

I would be the hot trailer and the milling hogs who will never
dive over the cliff. I would be the wheel the blonde girl turns,
her key in the lock, the cluttered table where she drops her purse,

the one who calls to her, darling, is it you, and yes, I would say,
yes, I'm home, and how are you, my love, how was your day?

The Recovery of Imaginary Friends

The guidebook of holy places lacks directions because
the places are holy, and when disturbed they move

somewhere else anyway. Still, consider the disturbing bison
on the cave wall, the reassuring handprint on the ceiling.

"We'll never know why the masks face inward," said
the tour guide, "but the people who made them know."

When the writer described her daughter's invisible friend,
I remembered my mother going on about Giffy,

my own lost companion, who did everything I shouldn't have.
All I know of him is what my mother tells the whole table

every other Christmas or so. Is it best to mourn
our imaginary friends or be glad to be shut of them?

I believe in holy places, both fixed and mobile,
and I believe in the lazy line of the Navajo rug.

I believe in Giffy, though he hasn't spoken to me since 1955.
I want the charismatic macrofauna to thrive

and the coral and honeybees, too. I want to bless
the unmedicated and the millionaire developers and to clean

the lead, mercury, and flame retardants from everybody's blood.
I want to know what Giffy's been up to, if he's happy,

stoned, depressed, working the night shift, solitary, gay,
pious, making cold calls or walking free and sweet through

some high canyon like the loose thread in a Navajo rug.

Late Psalm

Then David ran and stood over the Philistine, and took his sword and drew it out of his sheath, and killed him, and cut off his head with it.

—1 Samuel 17:51

It was dark when I left town and still dark when day had come, the
sky and trees dulled and damp.

I remembered the preacher: Consider David and Goliath, he said,
the two of them boasting of their strength and the God who
loved them, both of them warning that the other's sweet body
must fall bloody in the dust and be torn by dogs.

The children came up to hear the story told for them.

I drove through scant snow and the long spectacle of tree after
tree after tree, each brown and gray in its winter simplicity,
singular, alone and not alone. Then the Big Oak Church, like
another easy growth.

Couldn't we name all the churches after trees and creeks?

I wanted some sunshine, but that didn't mean I would get it. I
wanted some words as clear and sharp as swords, instead of a
sword.

Flurries and sunshine breaking through, and suddenly the word
sublime was in my head. I let a truck in ahead of me, passed
another, headed down the long, curving hill.

And Jackson Browne sang, "He rescued truth from beauty and
meaning from belief."

And the snowflakes seemed sparse enough to count, though I soon
gave up.

There are many worlds, and they are all this world, held apart by
thin braces of time and weather.

Sometimes you can spray all you want and let the wipers run, but the
windshield just won't come clean.

Besides forgiveness there must be something else, something like
abandon—going on without forgetting, without fear.

Abandoned, like the site of an ambush. Or the last camp on the way
to the ambush. Or the place where a few hungry people stayed
afterward, no water, no fire, just a place to lie down in the
snow.

An Hour

Good scholars are seldom good soldiers, or so the savage
and gentle heroes of Denmark decided early on their long way.

Thelwell thought it wrong to influence a child's mind
or to pull weeds: "I thought it unfair in me to prejudice

the soil toward roses & strawberries." Down the road
lived a courtesan of fairly good taste and a man convinced

he had a Bible in his head. The body is not corrupted
but by the soul, he insisted, painting the pickets again.

I cannot conceive the necessity, she said, for God to love me.
In such an hour, the mind floats with the evening winds

all over the dim valley. Threads that are roads, smooth fields,
the wrinkled hills where no one has walked for centuries.

But to be a scholar, a soldier, or a courtesan is seldom decided
at one's leisure. In the falling light, when the gentle,

savage heroes rise and float along the valley, I straighten up
to ease my back, lift my dirty hands from the roses.

Interior Colloquy in Glen Helen

How long do I have? Forty-two minutes. Is that a path or a watercourse?
Never mind. These rocks are really slick. Can I crawl through

the waterfall and into that little cave? Somebody must have.
What would James Wright say? Will I ever settle down?

What you mean "I," white man? Lunch will be good. Walk
a little more. Rhododendron, heavy bee making the blossoms nod.

Jet plane fills the whole glen with noise. Keep walking.
The real spring is above and behind the little falls I found last time,

the water breaks from its hidden routes and spins and rustles out
and along, the rocks and pool almost aglow, rust-orange,

three women pass and the tiny pool fills and spills over time
and again and a speck of water sails all the way to my book

and blurs the word *pool* and a music like water begins within me,
not head or heart but all through, any reason will do, any bad excuse,

a music not for or from me but all those beings shaking
their dumb selves awake in here, what can I do, they are starting

to rub their eyes, to straighten up, where are we, do you remember,
Constantinople, the dread sea, some boggy farm, the hut along

the dirt road, what happened, fire, mud, stones, does it matter,
oh it's you! And she is here, too, and William, and the redbird,

how many of us are there, do we need to count, do we need to talk?
Should we lie down together or take hands and amble away?

Some of us want to listen, some to cup hands and drink
from the cold spring. Some of us think we should sing.

Notes toward an Interrogation of Staged Violence

Here's your challenge: write a verse play in which nonviolence triumphs.

—ESR, 1/27/2006

Prelude:
Please be seated in this comfortable armchair. All questions will be asked in a calm and measured tone.
Would you prefer not to answer? Would you like a cup of tea, or a glass of whiskey, or a week in Cancun? Would you prefer that I punch you in the chops, or bomb an aspirin factory, or send the cruise missiles humming across the border like angry wasps ahead of the tanks and Humvees? I am only asking.

Propositions:
A story is not a war, but a creative alternative to stabbing your brother with a kitchen knife.
Time travel is indeed possible in the magic space of the stage.
Violence is available for deconstruction and assimilation.
Nothing is inevitable, even after it happens.
We must learn the power of powerless bodies.

Historical Note:
The martyrs eschewed all force except that which they elicited from their enemies, thereby a) heaping coals of fire or b) glowing in the fiery furnace or c) both creating and transcending the Bloody Theatre or d) . . .

Additional Propositions:
In stage combat, the victim controls the action.
Sound effects contribute verisimilitude.
The nonviolent spectator takes no pleasure in a whack or a stab.

The nonviolent spectator envisions glorious transformations and scenes of pastoral harmony way up and down the line.

Illustrations:
Her soul floats above the horrifying scene, almost free.
The crowd obscures the audience's view.
Hector drops the knife and weeps.
Angela achieves such sublime heights of serenity that she ascends to heaven in a narrow band of light.
Marilyn suddenly vanishes and there's a maple tree in her place, or a raccoon, or the attorney general with his blue curtain gone and the bare-breasted Spirit of Justice in glorious view.

Dialogue (suppressed):
All right, we've had it. You are neither natural nor inevitable. The restraints are for your own protection. We have assurances from our legal advisers. Those fingernails . . . One more opening in that tender flesh . . .

Proposed Approaches:
Abuse the puppet, and let Naomi put on something comfortable and sit down with a magazine.
The lead couple makes love onstage in such dazzling fashion that the alien cyborgs do a total makeover on their cubical spaceship and beg *us* to assimilate *them*.
Instead of letting the bastard cut out Philomel's tongue, change the whole crew into birds before anybody rapes anybody.
Everybody pauses at the crucial moment, exchanges glances fraught with significance, then goes out for Thai food or puts on the Beatles.
Hell, the Doobie Brothers.

Ode to Luna with Implausible Quotations

She was nothing like a lover. She was my temptation,
my temporary obligation, draped on the soft chair or under

the plant stand on the deck, a cat so fat she was like
a soft bowling ball with fuzzy extremities, always asleep

or wanting to go out or come in. At night she yowled
every twenty minutes, just loud enough to wake me.

Fear is the parent of earthly love, she indicated,
and he who will not bend to love must be subdued by fear.

Fine, I said, and went out on the deck. She stayed in.
Back in the world, enormous firepower was not making

the enemies go away, but here in the deep shade it was
almost comfortable, splashes of light in the meadow,

birdsong in the trees. If song is the symptom, is there
a disease? *You are the child of great mistakes,* I heard,

and now you must learn differently. I waited and tried
to listen. *The great one is undivided,* sang the birds;

he lives totally in every living thing. Inside, Luna was
spraddled on the floor, asleep again. *When you are living*

honestly with someone, she breathed, *there are moments*
when God quietly enters the room. Tonight she sleeps on the deck.

Astonishing Details of the Universe

Created things follow a pattern.
They do not know
rest.
—The Odes of Solomon, #16

1.
Every red-winged blackbird, every reed washed up against
the black shore, each thin new sparrow and pair

of white butterflies proclaims and embroiders in the same air.
If we asked, they might say, *Too many are neither awake nor asleep*.

2.
No one, sane or crazy, can sleep in the valleys of the clouds.
In the dawn, I rise and finger the foggy afterimages

of spacious rooms upstairs in the house, full of light
and antiques, burnished beds and dressers I could never afford.

3.
Try this for a story: George cries in his cradle.
George's mother loves him and cannot help him.

George marries and becomes a preacher. George falls
while rising from the toilet and never regains his strength.

George's children inherit the earth and rediscover
the blessed condition of the early church:

furtive, perplexed by rumors and apparitions,
they wrestle for splinters and bones.

4.
Beauty is not the problem or the answer.
My mother loves me and cannot help me now.

> *The gold coin of light is the sun,*
> *the gold coin of darkness is the night.*

There are more true words than there are bugs
in the Little Riley Creek.

> *He made the sun to clarify the day*
> *but evening blurs the face of the earth.*

The evidence is buried so deep
that we're all safe forever or lost for good.

> *Their alteration*
> *speaks the beauty of God.*

5.
Just off the familiar road is a clearing
where no one has walked in forty years

of light and shadow, dusks and dawns,
sleepy drivers following the curve

to the auto plant, passing the sumac and daylilies,
squinting into another sun.

The Poet on the Beaver Marsh

I was trying to write the song of bird wings and the grind
of shoes on gravel, to remember the notes I did not bring along,
to sing of the multiflora rose hedging the towpath, the canal

clogged with duckweed and pond lilies. I wanted to sing
of loud gossip and bar fights in the heron rookery,
of the trashed cars whose ghosts mingle with green frogs

and wood frogs and mosquitoes and the vast birds who circle
the trailer court and the sewage plant and alight with one last fish
for their gangly, insatiable chicks. I wanted to sing of the beavers

whose ancestors dammed the canal and pushed the water out
over acres of not much, changed all the plans and for once
were obliged instead of slaughtered. But when the enormous

breathing quickens in the dusk, I can't slap anything, or keep up,
or see in or out. The split trees say, *One more day without*
an explanation. They say, *Why so much fuss after the surrender?*

I meant to turn around; I meant to sing. Did I expect my beloved
to come running when my two notes echo so thin against
the boardwalk, the acres of thick water, the heavy thrumming

of the bullfrogs? She has already slid into the damp vinyl
of the '63 Impala, slammed the door, rolled down her window,
and taken the smoke from the hand of the dark-eyed boy

who lives in the narrowest trailer on the lot. He laughs
and touches her thigh, pulls at the gearshift, guns the engine,
and gravel erupts and the heavy car spins away, all its lights out.

February Report on Conditions in the Interior

1. I was either too early or too late again this morning, but the sun had me covered.
2. The tips of Scotch pine littering the backyard have stayed green for weeks. I still don't know if the wind or some demented squirrel took them down.
3. Last night the neighbor on the corner drove her old Buick up over the curb and parked on her own grass again.
4. Last week in Samarra, our guys drove their Humvee back to base with two dead insurgents strapped to the hood like deer.
5. The square of plywood nailed over the bottom half of the lime-green garage's broken window years ago is holding.
6. The three strange angels have not been seen in weeks.
7. No snow since December, and the ice shelves along the creek bank are shrinking and cracking.
8. Agonizing reappraisals of the true, the good, and the right continue.
9. Somebody sawed the big fallen limb into lengths just right for burning, then left them on the brown grass like a puzzle for dummies.
10. Everybody I know still showers completely naked. As far as I know.
11. *There is no one sleeping,* wrote Tony Hoagland.
12. I met him once in a diner in Baltimore, which is nowhere near Samarra.
13. *There is no one sleeping,* he wrote, *who does not dream of being touched.*
14. The leftover bale of straw is still at the edge of the garden, slowly and irreversibly becoming something else.
15. *A crucial dimension is one of humility,* wrote my smart friend.
16. *The gospels can be read as an anamnesis of blindness,* wrote his smart friend.
17. The president is threatening veto, but his minions are still restless.
18. The skaters are beautiful, strong, and angry.
19. Death said, "I was surprised to see your servant here in Baghdad, for tonight I must meet him in Samarra."

20. My eyes feel better since I've been using the lotion.
21. I can't lose those three Christmas pounds, though I've been riding the cursed bike every night.
22. Maybe tomorrow my heart will break out, or open, or down.
23. Maybe two riders are approaching and the wind will begin to howl.
24. Maybe my soul will grow so slender it can slip between sash and frame and enter the seamless blue.
25. A great golden dome was shattered yesterday in Samarra.
26. *Want to live forever?* the e-mail asks, but the message is empty.
27. Tonight we start to build another dome, in the secret place where the gospel is always clear and silent.
28. The ducks are still on the pond.

Hum

The car purrs along at seventy-two, engine noise lost in the whisper of wind and the music. I love to hit the Volvo's cruise control and turn up the stereo and roll along alone, checking the mirrors, the gauges, letting my thoughts go long and loose, knowing it'll be hours on the road and that I can stop for coffee and gas and to pee whenever I feel like it, that I have credit cards and cash and extra oil in the trunk just in case.

Between my mushy tree-hugger tendencies and my friends buying gas-electric hybrids, I'm a little guilty about the S90, which gets twenty-seven miles to a gallon at best. But because it had been badly mistreated we got it way cheap, and having worked it all over with my son I know it better than any machine and most of the people that I've ever met. It still has its quirks and mysteries, trembles a little at idle, uses too much oil, shakes sometimes when you hit the brakes. But at seventy it rides like a dream, smooth and steady, ready to carry me down the longest road and into the deepest sunset.

I go days on end and never get in a car, walking to work as I do, so I love to put my bag and books in the back, arrange my coffee mug and case of CDs and map and head off to play poet somewhere. It feels good to call off classes, give the students some token work to do, get up earlier or later than usual, and hit the road, knowing I'll be greeted and fed, paid attention and shown to a good bed.

But all that is just backdrop for the pleasure of humming along on whichever interchangeable Midwestern interstate it is. I emerge from driving reveries not knowing where in the world I am, except that I am in the small private space of the car, within the whirring, complicated, efficient machine that bears me along the way I used to think my soul was carried around by my body.

A few hours and I drift free from my body, cushioned in the leather seat, the temperature steady, nothing to do besides keep a hand on the wheel and stay between the lines. I snatch every glimpse I can of what's beyond the shoulders of the road, among the trees, in the sky.

The car is the body and the body is the soul and the soul is no longer inside the body but floating, flying, slipping through the window to lick at the air like a golden retriever, its wisps and tatters trailing wildly in the wind of passage.

Where Water Finds an Edge

—Blue Hen Falls, June 2004

Nothing like a careful, thorough plan with one large error.
Too dark under the trees, too many roots—

we must turn back. Rocks piled around like bad excuses,
like my father's brow as he gently explains

just how deep and wide my screwup is. I stumble
for a place to sit, break through a thin sheet of shale.

Even the skin of the earth can't be trusted.
Every splash is a sign; not one is a word.

But we know the light was hiding all these stars.
We need the dark because it makes us clumsy,

because it makes us forget the banks
we are rushing between, muttering about hymns

and women while the falls spill out before us.
We will not need to be ready to tumble down.

We will shine and shout, and all the damage
will be forgotten soon. The water is not wounded

by its breathless journey, it bears its troubles lightly,
it does not falter as the full night arrives.

And the hard ledges glow, long after all else is lost.

Firefly

I want to find the room where my father is sleeping,
take his hand and wake him. I will say I am sorry

to have come so late, after all the other children.
I will ask about his heart and his dreams,

apologize for disturbing his rest. I want to drive there
faster than anybody, but I am not even on the way home.

The masters say all is one, but I am five hundred miles away,
studying the alphabet of broken trees

and the gorgeous dusk of the beaver marsh.
The masters say nothing is separate, but I am lost

among the lilies, the needly mosquitoes, the slow tenderness
of the fireflies. I will leave tomorrow if need be.

Tonight I will dream of the great healing,
and the night will be warm with the hum of fireflies,

the chir and splish of the beavers fitting one more stick,
one more slap of mud into the mile-long dam.

II

Rules (Observed and Unwritten) for Hot Sundays in the Heart of the Empire

1: When the hummingbirds pass up the red sugar water to sip from the milkweed and clover at the fringes of the woods, it's hot.

2: The longer the man on cable takes to answer, the more chance he's blowing smoke.

3: The body knows what it needs, though it tends to mumble.

4: When a scruffy cardinal checks all around then sneaks in to peck at the mixed seed, it's time for a bike ride.

5: If the creek is shallow enough to ford with dry feet, it's time for a rain.

6: That doesn't mean it will rain.

7: If a yellow cat and two rabbits cross your path, the gears of the cosmos are about to groan and wrench us into the final transformation.

7a: Or else not.

8: Some people get all warm when a petty broken rule enables them to wax effusive on the need for order and the pain they feel as they feed the poor sucker into the chipper.

9: Given that mosquitoes like certain missiles are heat-seeking, only some kind of fool would get all sweaty and then sit down in the weeds by the sluggish creek.

10: The shoreline rocks are parched and pale, but they know it wasn't always this way and won't be again, and so they pulse with the same wild patience they bore when people like us were still learning to flake arrowheads.

11: An equation re the current value of our dead vs. their dead is under development.

12: While the dead are sometimes proud and often tersely eloquent, not one has yet shown true gratitude.

13: Until further notice, you may, for planning purposes, use the ratio 1:1.

14: The first days are not, in fact, the hardest days.

The Vice President for Obscure Relations Rises to Offer Something Resembling an Explanation

Spiders prowl the house, and the groundhog grumbles
under the deck. Still, God's treasury of virtues expands

every evening by three or four minutes.
The radical diminution of flat tires is a motive

for one sort of hope. The ballots will soon be in your hands,
the little fish and old leaves mingle in the quarry,

the fluid in the barrel of the pen is clear but turns dark
on the page, a black not quite black.

These lessons can be traced on the empty loom,
can be read for their solemn relevance

even while prodigals and memories escape in all directions.
The man whose name is Bible has been working late.

We could all be meeting every night, or shoveling coal
for a living, or getting paid like the day care workers

whose charges are, after all, the future.
We propose to create a cap on future tergiversations

unless all hell breaks loose
and the Hell Back into Place Plan becomes necessary,

in which case you will all be notified at once.
Keep these with you at all times.

Meditation on Brilliance, Absinthe, Love, and Power

I must tell you I never think of poetry as anything but a loving power.
—Donald Revell

The brilliant dead poet looked first, always, for something fun.
Then he threw out everything not absolutely true.
He never forgot those liquid nights, his friends at the rough table.

Somehow the voice penetrated the steely official jaw:
We reject this charge, and your mama, too.
We want every single allegation out of town by sundown.

The stars are still there in the day sky
with the climbing moon and the declining sun,
one cold coin, one hot one.

Like God, this poem is still unfinished.
I used no absinthe in its construction,
although I stole and altered without remorse.

I echoed the cry of the bat, which I could not hear.
I secured the smoking wreckage
and offered the most generous of terms.

This poem was born far from the front lines.
It nursed at the generous breasts of the empire.

This poem has taken no position
on those little-known, abandoned armies
who were forced to choose cannibalism or starvation.

What is it worth, to have had brilliant friends
and been brilliant among them?

The soldier shot his friend, then wept.
He accepted the left hand, weeping.

A serious moment for the match, said the poet,
is when it bursts into flame.

God help me, said the mighty Patton, *but I love it.*

Tales of Feeble and Bitter Boys

Winter breaks up early on the Elkhart River
where the ice is never safe. Years ago, we strolled
under the bitter moon, while the dark fish

plotted and assembled below. We knew we were
too smart to die, too beloved by our mothers
to fall through anything. But that was before

the debacle, before the coffeehouses, before
the dam was renovated, then destroyed
under the Apocalyptic Preventive Maintenance Act.

We all wore purple to the wake, not wanting God
to be pissed. We strutted in sadly, even Ishmael
whose pockets were full of water and sand.

We kept saying, *We only are left alive to tell thee.*
We sat together and lonely in the back row, watching
the girls in their pale dresses whisper each to each,

knowing that they were not whispering our names.

What We Said When We Talked All Day

The psychic with the hazy eyes said: When I saw Gabriel's face, I was thrown to the floor, flattened by beauty.

The monastic visitor said: These are the two prongs of a soulful person. Can fat people be spiritually mature? As a scientist, any failure of quantification threatens to fling me into crisis. It's not easy to preach from the middle of the Dark Night.

While we collect the offering, please indicate the extent of your agreement with these statements:

> There are people I find physically repulsive.
> I really would like to have sex with many persons.
> I expect others to remember the favors I do them.
> I find nature ugly and cruel.
> Reading scripture inspires me about as much as reading the phone book.
> I feel a strong desire to move into a body without external genitalia.

The professor of angelic needlework said: I love the idea that this angel is mine, and it's Christian not to share it with anybody. You have your own. Mine is named Irving.

The man in the blue gloom said: It now seems God left town without telling me goodbye. My heart does not leap up. Those ahead of me on the path are all wretches and hypocrites. When I sit still the mud settles, and then I get sleepy and hungry. My spiritual mentor is too critical and not so holy as he thinks. In times of meditation, I find myself pondering the many persons I would rejoice to discover in my bed.

The psychic said: Being blind is nothing. It's these people dropping dead that drive me nuts.

Heresy in Ohio, or What I Learned at Books on Main

The Secret is sacred, but it is also somewhat ridiculous.
—Jorge Luis Borges, "The Sect of the Phoenix"

Writing vast books, Borges noted, is hard work for small reward:
"I have preferred to write notes on imaginary books."

Michael Servetus was burned slowly in John Calvin's Geneva,
his heretical *Restitutio* at his side. Calvin had wanted him killed

but more humanely. After denying the doctrine of the Trinity,
Servetus described precisely how blood flows from heart to lungs,

decades before anyone else. Three copies of his book survived.
At Books on Main, I got Borges and cyberpunk, Le Guin

and Mary Oliver and Thomas Merton, all for $22.63. I have
no work this afternoon, a car, and a kitchen full of food.

The surplus is gone, but we have Baghdad and the secret,
which is like the thousand flags along Main Street,

holy and self-indulgent, sacred and ridiculous.
Calvin asked Servetus: "How, unhappy man, if any one

strike the pavement with his foot and say that he tramples
on thy God, wouldst thou not be horrified?"

And Servetus: "I have no doubt that this bench, and this buffet,
and all you can show me, are of the substance of God."

Note from the Week after Next

The dawn is gray now, night and day, and we are no more pleased than the roosters and the finches.

Their whistles and squawks annoyed us, especially when we had frittered the night away with bottles and companions, but now we have lost even the sad thrill of carousing while the honest folk drowse.

The solid citizens have started to show up at Wal-Mart at all hours, to fill their carts with lawn ornaments, wrapping paper, bottles of oil treatment. They haunt the laundromats, smoke in clumps on street corners, astonished by their own transgressions.

The songbirds, herons, and crows gather unevenly on the public lawns, exchanging conspiratorial chirps and flutters.

Before he disappeared, the secretary of hours insisted that the absence of both sun and darkness was neither unexpected nor cause for alarm. Given the vicious and barbaric nature of our enemies, he stated, the casualty level is tragic but within acceptable parameters. He pledged firm action, soon.

Rumors of crash programs—to adjust the rate of continental drift, to utilize vast engines to reshape certain orbits, to rekindle subtle stellar processes—spring up like mushrooms and blacken just as fast.

Each time we assemble, at intervals ever more arbitrary, a few more are coughing quietly into white rags.

Signature, or Jonathan Edwards and Joe Walsh Meet in the Electric Brew

Signing two hundred times in a row will reveal the weak spots in any soul.
What hope can there be for a middle-aged guy who can't make

a decent *G* or a *y* that doesn't twist this way or the other?
If I could please myself just once, I'd know what to aim for,

but over and over it's no, not quite. I'm no closer to getting
it right than the poor little guy whose mother just shoved him away

for interrupting—he stuck his thumb in his mouth and wandered off
to buy candy or drugs or meet some stranger in the bathroom.

We're one step from falling through the rotten cover of the world,
always, and that's why I go on about the grammar of trees

and earning the ending and how to say *I am sad and the world*
is cold, my house is poor and my car is old in a pleasingly adept

and grounded fashion, e.g., *The lovely women have cell phones*
pressed to their ears, or *All the roses and whisky in Goshen*

barely got me through last night. No amount of coffee
will realign the nubbly ions of my blood. The world hurls itself

through space at least five ways at once and not only is the past
gone, it's way the hell over there, too. I can't complain,

but sometimes I still do. Even my angry love of the seminal
rock musicians of the last century is dissolving in apocalyptic

nostalgia as some jerked-over band sings “Norwegian Wood”
in French while the Mountaineers and Armadas fight it out

on the streets and the pale leaves of the sidewalk trees
signal wildly at the wild wind, hey, did we sign up for this?

When Madonna Met Menno

"You're a slut," he said, "but God loves you anyway."
She took a long pull on her beer. "Don't be simple,"
she said. "I was a Catholic schoolgirl. I've known that
since I was twelve." She was all knees and ankles,

and he was a river toad, the two of them crammed
into a tiny booth among the hard-drinking yuppies.
"Besides, I've got babies now," she said, "and all that
whore stuff was for sales anyway." "I know what you mean,"

said Menno. "Most of my whoring was for the Church,
but I think I gave it up too soon." He took an even
longer pull on his beer. "I did a lot of brooding
about the Blessed Mary back then," he said. "I decided

that Jesus slid out of her like a seed through a tube.
She was just a vase for the beautiful flower." "What a load,"
said Madonna. "Mary was Jesus, and he was her, too."
"Yeah, I've been wrong before," said Menno. "You want

a basket of fries, another beer?" They could feel the subway
underneath them, a heavy snake hauling another wave
of puzzled souls from there to elsewhere. "No," she said,
"the kids will be home. Time to cross the river."

The Visiting Poet Blunders through His Own Assignment

as chaff lifts toward God.
—Julia Kasdorf, "Mennonites"

I disobeyed the instructions, but only to prowl and supervise.
I remembered the mercy of my mother's gentle scowl.

J. always said she was a wild driver, but I figured she was blowing smoke
until she veered past the *No Entrance* sign and floored it.

After two Amish ales, C. deemed this gesture to be fully postmodern
in its imbricative eschewal of rational metanarrative.

I walked the long way around the dredged Lake Placida,
past the planted cattails: the geese are afraid of sharp teeth hiding,

D. explained, so they take their goose crap elsewhere.
"When you run out of paint, you quit painting, " E. always said.

Truth, said N., is a soured metaphor, its date lapsed centuries ago.
He demanded his bowel movements be boxed, dated, stacked

along the wall like rations for the pending death of symbolism.
But the kids in their sweatshirts predicted nothing;

they scrawled earnestly until it was time for the next class,
then bolted from the meetinghouse without a qualm or a word.

If I had followed the rules, I would have three slips
of borrowed paper, I'd have somebody's fragrant words

to lay down among my muddled notes
like a bridge from the marsh to the forest,

like women who find themselves perplexed and naked
in dreams they know are not their own.

And the yellow light would keep playing in the leaves
and wandering into the big plain room, around

and about us, and like these dust motes we would rise
and swirl toward heaven from the planked and square-nailed floor.

Praise Is a Language

The young preacher said so and then hurried on, and the girls
who had led the praise songs nodded and whispered in the front pew,
but wait, I muttered in my head, if praise is a language then what

can we use it to say? How widely is it spoken, and should we maybe
listen instead of talking so much? I have seen praise glowing
in the cornstalks glazed with mud and snow. I have heard

the fine twigs of the sickly high tree outside my fourth-floor
window sifting the unsteady wind. I have taken the stairs
two at a time and groped for my key and dreamed that

the language of praise might launch itself across the wide skies,
cross vacuums and voids like radio or photons, carry some
wild packet of data and yearning that would cause the High One

suddenly to relent, to pass out the sports cars and the answer keys,
to sit down alone and together with us all and tenderly explain
the languages of bullies, traffic, RPGs, anthrax, patriarchy,

and cholesterol, propound in words glowing and clear the need
for better and more detailed articulations of the High One's
splendor, grandeur, majesty, and might, for the pretty good guitar

strummed nearly in time, for the blonde girl who sweetly sang
Father, Father as the rest of us tried to follow the tune.

Notes toward Local Representation of Complex Linguistic Events

A. This is the best book: it echoes our slogan, our mission statement,
and my personal mantra, which I must never reveal. I will now
pray in another language. Listen, and dream you have entered

the smoky heaven where we will know and be known.
B. The brilliant Chinese general held off the Japanese for years.
Finally they agreed to parley. He sketched the river for them,

and though he was illiterate he signed his name, beautifully
but incorrectly. When they pointed out his mistake, he said,
I will not give you anything that is not laden with error.

C. Here is the update: in the cold sunshine, the brown creek
rushes north. Old leaves lie scattered under the bare trees.
The bridge is encrusted but passable. The future university

will look like a chocolate cake, or a wrecked hoop
with a caution sign below, or a gorgeously tangled Slinky.
D. Answer these questions in complete sentences:

1. Which of these canny paragraphs do you least deplore?
2. When you hear the word "share" used to mean "speak,"
   do the hairs on your neck prickle?
3. When you hear "realignment of funds," does your heart leap
   up?

E. My heart leaps up when I hear "concluding remarks." It does
not leap when I hear "gold-plated decision." What if all the air
in the room suddenly fell to the floor? If the key to the next life

fell into your hands? Imagine that all the light in town gathered
into a crackling sphere and slid slowly, slowly toward your head.
Would you cry out in joy, or run away? F. I know what the plan

is not. I find I'm not across the river as much as I would like.
I cannot emphasize this enough. I see the forty-eight people
who are meeting to plan. I see the dean duck out the door.

Futurism in the Black Swamp

Jagged split ends of trunk like coarse feathers,
fallen but still attached. What isn't memory, reverie,
stark guesswork, or wishful thinking? If I is an other,

a puzzle, a fiction, why am I sweating so much ?
The lost leaves rattle, offer their thin musk.
Let's hear it for speed, said Marinetti, still buzzing

with the postaccident rush. Let's hear it for hot cars
and bullets. War will make us clean. I've had
those days, too. Today my sore heel barely hurt.

Today I only heard about a few people who got
blown up. I doubt I love poetry more than my own
sweet flesh or the sound of my woman singing.

One winter, some drunk in an old Chevy knocked
my sister's shed right off its foundation
trying to drive into Riley Creek, backed out

and muddled his way to the quarry, where he left
the car sideways on the ice and took off for Van Wert
without even stripping the plates. They hauled

him back babbling about the sanity of utter restlessness,
the bankruptcy of yesterday, the solemn duty
of the artist to be drunk and out on the ice.

His insurance never paid up. Finally, Kate and my dad
and Joel and me got some pipe and two big pry bars,
hauled and rolled the shed square, nailed the sprung

siding down, threw some junk away, put the mower,
the potting soil, the hose, and the lawn chairs
back inside, and closed the doors up tight.

Structural Adjustments to Maintain Growth Will Be Necessary

Anger is more useful than despair, I heard last night,
but that was just the Terminator speaking, and he knew
the missiles were bound to fly anyway. All he wanted

was to keep the right people around to fight later, his own
robotic self not included. Anyway, a martyr now and then
is good for any group struggling against long odds,

and everybody dies, too cool to be forgotten or not.
Lately I hear myself say the most confusing things,
sing the weirdest songs I know without fumbling

the chords, as if my inner obstacles have finally collapsed.
A little kindly notice and you start thinking that people
who sit around polished tables give a heavy crap about

who speaks prettily and whose interior monologue went sour
a year ago. It's all shoulders and slopes, angles and appropriate
utterance. You can enter the office and sit down; you can wax

eloquent or crude or sweet in any language except effective.
Less is more. The pruned tree grows more shapely
and alluring by the day. The sawn limbs burn so gaily,

launch out so freely into the next life while we dance,
dance around them, howl and praise our mighty God
for the mercy he has shown us, hallelujah, amen.

Letter with Melody and Fall from Chair

There is so much to explain. First, I was one of those farm boys
with the hard and horny hands, the ones the farm girls feared

and disdained. For years, I tried to stay on nodding terms
with the people I used to be. Then I walked out of the temple,

and my guide discoursed upon the elephant, its mighty tusks,
its shoulders like boulders. But no, that wasn't me.

Like a dream, this world is best recorded the minute we wake up.
The strong woman said, *The I is a dark bar, a shadow on the page.*

She said, *Style is all a matter of rhythm, which makes a shape*
in the mind. Then she said, *Well, I'm going,* and I let her walk.

When the verse ended, the fiddle picked up the melody,
and what I knew seemed a fog that was just about to clear.

Is anything more authentic than feeling like an imposter?
Most facts can be worried into fiction. The two old men said,

How dare you travel on your own? and just to say something,
I said, *God will protect me.* My wife and I drove around Haarlem

for a baffled hour before we figured out that our map had south
at the top. He said, *What the reader wants is an unbroken dream,*

and I fell off the chair. It’s like *Fight Club:* no rules,
months of concrete and bruises, and it turns out

your mind has been beating up your face all the time.
Forget the notes and write to your unknown friends.

Forget about sitting, forget about travel. Wait for the music.
Fall out of your body. Another will be waiting.

III

Dark Man Blues

Who is the man in dark clothes walking
the woods along the path, beside us, not with us?

Below the dam, the long heron, the selfish messenger,
stalks his late dinner in the shallows.

I am learning what the catalpa knows,
the seedy cousin of the one outside my childhood window,

its rattly long pods like rations for the next life.
In the dry marsh, last year's twisted arrangements

remain in place, and the small creatures wait for news.
Rivers have vanished suddenly, but not our rivers,

and the broken cities are still far away.
The true dark has not fallen for fifty-two years,

but the spring dusk comes early to the woods
and Jupiter finds a way through the clouds,

high and sharp as the bells striking a quarter past.
Back at the dam, all the water is still willing to go down.

The Song of the Weed Witch

No ideas but . . .
—William Carlos Williams

I could walk up or down the creek, but I stop. So little time.
Here's the strainer someone left on the rocks, the air
so damp it's one degree from fog. Here's the weed

rooted somehow in the mossy boulder, almost ready to seed.
Despite much instruction, I've never mastered the simple
clear explanation. I've never figured out how to put ideas

in things. In this simple, indescribably deep forest,
I remember last night when we were suddenly talking
about what might survive our bodies, and my new friend said,

I could go to church if I didn't have to believe *all that stuff,*
and I said I knew what she meant. But the beer was gone,
and we were tired. I got in the car, and the singer sang

Three crosses in a copse of trees, a long way from Calvary,
and I found my room, slept, woke into another
irrevocable and precious day and put not one idea

into a thing. I spoke mostly to the one inside who listens darkly
to my obnoxious supplementary monologues, the one
who says very little beyond *walk, then* and *sit here*

and *listen* and *wait.* There are many things—the mossy boulder,
a dead leaf sprawled on it, some wispy grass, lichens,
a foot-tall weed, almost ready to seed—and not an idea

in the whole passel. Where the creek turns, a mist rose or lowered
or gathered. The whole forest spun without moving
and hummed without noise, simple and clear and enormous.

All these adjectives must die, I know, and be flung
on a heap like the honeysuckle that the weed witch is clearing
to let the natives flourish—skunk cabbage, spicebush,

jack-in-the-pulpit. I am a native but not exactly at home,
so I listened to the nearby water and the distant water,
and a drop fell on my shoulder like a reason to turn.

June Report with Suppressed Geese and Sweatbees

Whoever built all these fine solid dwellings is too rich to even need them.

A few locals whiz past in their hard-shelled travel gear.

My project to learn all the names has once again faltered.

Cattails, yes, and the white-blossomed bushes look like spirea, but does that grow wild? And the long purple flower stalks—blue vervain? Blazing star? And that low-profiled pond-swimmer, could it be a turtle? a muskrat? an unearthly visitor?

Not to mention the invisible bird crying *Dee-dee-dee! Dee-dee-dee!* with absolute conviction.

Notwithstanding the clouds and their murky yet definite silence.

And the breeze that builds and builds from the south, and the poplar leaves that translate every nudge and nuance into their own tongue, and the gust from the west, as if some covert parley of the winds has begun.

And now two swifts pluck lunch from the pond without alighting, and one great heron rolls somber and strong above us all.

What if every body carries the whole world? Not in its arms like a mother, not on its back like the turtle groaning far below in that other story.

No, the way an old man can carry a thousand stories and a million
songs, whether or not anyone asks to hear them.

What if all we need is to find one more clue? Or give up one more
weak desire? Or refuse to give up anything?

Or leap for once and all on the muscular neck of the dark snake of
the world and ride ride ride into the clouds, into the dirt, into
the blank eye of the pond?

Some Things of This World

Hemlock Ravine filled with beeches
slate deerflies ferns spicebush

two big battered red maples lean
like a couple married sixty years
forty of them happy

Horsefly whose lifework is to chase walkers
off the bridge

The perfect web could be a target
or a trail marker but notice
the genius pulsing at its center

There are ghosts older than the wisest tree
quicker than the shyest bird
more remote than the last leaf on the highest limb
closer than the shoots pushing brave and bedraggled
from a root in the middle of the trail

How many intricate tons of matter
raised up by sunlight into sunlight
how many more breathing and working in the dirt

Lilies tread water
dreaming of boats
deerfly bites my left arm
bullfrog dives

Beloved
just off the trail
where the white sun was firing a young beech
I saw you

Report on Recent Activities in Austin (Selected)

I watched the bats boil distant and otherworldly from under the
bridge

J discovered she'd booked the wrong flight and couldn't leave till
Monday and left several wild messages on my cell phone

Later I left the stupid thing at airport security after noticing a dish
full of pens and change somebody else had left behind and
barely quashing the impulse to jam it all into my pocket

In between I walked among the tattoo parlors and T-shirt shops and
empty bars in the hot quiet afternoon and then again late and
dark, the streets jammed with young drunks and an enormous
stretch Hummer, a door flung open, a woman in flowing dress
crouched inside—*blow job,* I said, *I think she's throwing up,* J
said, but we didn't stay to find out

And I laughed and ate and drank in the noisy rooms where my ears
and soul were dented and bruised by all the good cheer and
shameless butt-kissing, the way too much water from the hose
will flatten the new tomatoes

We waited on the bridge as the sun glumly abandoned the city, not
sure where to be or what to watch

I couldn't get the damn cell phone to ring, but when we finally found
each other J told the story pluckily and we all told her how
much fun she could have with a free day in the city

I walked her back to her hotel through the mostly happy drunks and
some guy trashed on a bad powder tried to talk to us, *Cheers,*
he said, and I turned away and thought we'd lost him but he
followed, saying, *Where are we? What is this?* until we walked
away fast

J said, Wait, why did I ask *you* to walk me, you're such a pacifist,
what are you going to do, ask to be beaten up and then burned
at the stake?

So I made my standard promises and remembered hearing that
war poetry was the fitting and proper genre for the humdrum
brutality of America

And the bats swept out in a vast spidery ribbon of need and invisible
sound, their hunger and delight carried them in skeins and
pulls across the darkening sky, a huge scarf loosely knitted of
fur and bones and sharp small teeth

And even in their numberless numbers they covered only a small arc
of the sky, which accepted their passage with neither hunger
nor delight

Small World

Not far off the path is a tiny galaxy, no stars
but streaks of light dangled and glancing

in the hollow of three twigs—how to make
something of almost nothing. When the sun fades,

it dulls to a fog, half a breath on an absent mirror.
Tattered remains hang below, lines from a fouled parachute.

But the flyer is home and dry, not diving
but dangling upside down by his eight toes,

a mean god hanging from the roof
of a very small heaven, a god so petty

his only thought is to make one convert a day,
stun him and wrap him and slowly suck him dry.

Day at the Pond without Geese

A good day for late wildflowers—daisies and burrs
leaned out into the path for a better view, brilliant

blue somethings with tiny blooms on tall stalks.
A good day for a young dog's yapping, the splish

of a muskrat, thin gold of poplar leaves screening
the low sun. At the end of a lush summer, not much

has changed. The latest suicide bomber was nearly
done with law school. The enemy shot her brother.

Afterwards her head was found on the floor
of the restaurant in Haifa, black hair still flowing.

Like most men in such times, I want to give advice.
The pond is pretty in its small way, trees still green,

a bank of cattails, water echoing blurry greens and sky,
for once no geese to harry and complicate things.

Two quiet wrens, that dog yelping stupidly,
and a crow way off to the east. Like most men,

I think I'm smarter than most men. I dream of women
even when I'm awake. If I sit long enough, the trees

or the water will surely tell me something. A woman
passes, explaining to her cell phone as she walks.

As far as I can see, everything is calm as Eden.
Her black hair, flowing like the night.

On the Day I Meant to Leave Town

Here inside the box of my office, I'm warm and safe and have the phone, the mouse and screen, two thousand books and magazines give or take, coffee, a hidden candy stash. And more—a goose feather, a dozen small stones, a deer mandible with three molars still clinging.

Ice pitters on the window, and the spider plant presses itself that way, though it would die if its desire were granted.

The sleety rain has been falling all day, hesitant but never ceasing. All morning the streets and sidewalks kept melting off, but the cars grew an extra hard layer, and the trees and even the grass hunched in their shining coats as though worried by this new and heavy gloss, as if they knew beauty is no grand gift, as if they knew my sweet blonde cousin, who at fifteen was stunning every boy in range. Two years later, she was stuck in a bad apartment with a pretty, whiny baby and a handsome absent dirtbag of a guy.

In here, the weather hasn't changed in months. Sleet spatters on the screen, some of it sticks, and a pattern gathers up from the southeast corner, knurled like the yellow glass in the church of my youth, as fancy as we dared to make it.

Horrible, said the weatherman.

My body aches like I'm wearing a yoke, you said, *but I would hate to see you out in this.*

So would I. I'm not going anywhere.

When Superman faced a wall he couldn't just knock down, he was stumped. Finally, though, he eased himself up to it and just *oozed* his way through, gently, no doubt slipping his stringy particles in and out of all the others . . . somehow.

This was the George Reeves black-and-white fifties Superman, sturdy but hardly buff, more convincing as Clark Kent than in his suit and cape.

Yet he defended truth, justice, and the American way and was never defeated, though often dependent on plot twists invented by underpaid blacklisted screenwriters, also working under false identities, whose views on the phrase "American way" and the penetration of impenetrable walls might reward further contemplation.

My neck's been sore for weeks, but I keep telling myself that it's very slowly getting better.

The high branches rock and sway, glazed thick as pretzels dipped in white chocolate, holding up as best they can.

Lunch Poem at Snow Road

We say God and the imagination are one . . .
—Wallace Stevens

The hummers don't even care
when I come out through the door.

And those high wisps of cloud head north
as if they had an appointment

as two hawks swoop in the meadow
and are gone. And because it's lunch time,

I can say anything. Imagine my wife
walking home to eat, crossing

the hot streets of our town,
choosing the shade when she can.

Her headache's better today,
I hope. Let her keep walking,

enter the house, riffle through the mail.
I can imagine anything today,

I can remember my very first day,
how spirit and body slid together

like two hands joining. I remember
the cool flame that washed

and fused them into one, as God
and the imagination might be one,

as the bee smacks hard
at the window and falls to the deck

and lies buzzing incredulously
until it finds its wings and flies off

and does it once more to be sure.

Cuyahoga Rules

The post is hot, sun-warmed on my back,
the golden gorgeous evening flows over the park

on the Crooked River, the swallows a-twitter,
poplars whispering, a fly circling. By now

it feels like home—no, like camp, the place
you know you can't stay. But what could be better

than to walk in the woods with a clutch
of friendly strangers who know the things I love,

who tell us all *every thing curls inward, like snakes,*
or *notice this birdfoot trefoil* or *never look away*

from the flower until you have seen your face.
Every bird has its own song and at least three names,

and somebody here knows at least two of them.
All I need to do is walk out with the rest

and watch with as much of my soul and body
as I can get to wake up, listen close, and tell

every secret I can think of, true or not.
Hear the ovenbird, hear the vireo, says the voice,

and inside some room deep in my body
a small light flickers on and then steadies.

Settle

What the ego wants is tiny compared to what the soul wants.
—Marion Woodman

I.
It's fine that the trees are scrubby and the ground
low and mucky, it's all right that the clean pond is kept

that way by buzzing pumps and heavy berms that wall
it off from the cattails and the lily swamps. There are

the brilliant purple flowers at water's edge, the bee's nest
big as a football high in a tree. There's the resident heron

flapping at the tree-rim, bound elsewhere. If I could
settle somewhere I'd be happy, twenty minutes, ten,

any log or bank where I could watch and wait
without this buzzing at my ears and elbows.

It wasn't so long ago, six, eight thousand years,
that my people didn't have houses at all.

Where did they shelter? What poems did they make?
Did they ever find an easy place and stay there, quiet,

until their souls could settle and their waters clear?

II.
Thursday morning, not cool but the sun shifts
in the new growth and at marsh edge the spindly willow

is full of loud birds and three crows bob and weave
like happy boys above the lilies, and even the granular

and modest duckweed seems satisfied. I hear that in cities
people are choking themselves near death because

they want so much, or so little. The hummingbird
wants time for four good drinks. I want to go so thin

and light that the deerflies won't even notice me. I want
to sail into the thick woods, to nuzzle through the branches,

to touch the flicker and the ovenbird so gently
that nothing is disturbed, to spread my narrow sails

and drink all day with the maple and the beech,
the poplar and the elm, and talk our rustling talk

all through the wild dark evening when
the cold wind from Canada blows through at last.

Letter to Students Gone for Summer

In the sunny afternoon, I walked home past the lagoon, thinking of our evening walks, how we would try to slow down, to be quiet, to see. The new leaves unfold everywhere now, almost hiding the trees the ice storm broke and the ruts we dug, dragging off the deadfalls.

Tiny daisies bloom along the path, and new poison ivy grows below the steps down to the creek. I would have brought you here, but there wasn't room for us all. The water is low and as clear as it ever gets, slipping over its stones like a dancer.

What else is new? The bastards and the unholy fools still run most of the world. My life is still calm and easy. It makes no kind of sense. Birds sing from every side, and two ducks zoom downstream, climb through the trees like quiet fighter jets. For all they know, this is the best of all the worlds. For all I know, this is the world of all the best birds, and God the great heron cares nothing about me, the ants, or the garlic mustard.

In that stuffy classroom, I would say *write now* and listen to the rustle of pens and pencils. It was like listening to birds invent new songs, like watching those films of flowers unfolding. Sometimes a face slipped so open that I had to turn away not to melt or go blind.

Wind tips the shadow of a young maple back and forth over my page, the fish strike at insects skimming the pool upstream, the mistuned pickup rackets away. We will never all be in the same room again, but I sit here with all of you in my mind, dreaming that the words that will save us are just two steps ahead.

We Go Out Searching for Sermons in Stone

The slender branch lifts in the wind as the tour guide explains
at length what the world will teach. Turkeytail fungus won't hurt
this dead tree or any other. See the bark-colored moth,

a wing missing. Notice the three-legged toad, the tracks
of deer and golf carts, the stump sprouts of the tulip poplar,
stubborn but doomed. A plant without a face is hard to name.

Tired of looking where I'm told, sick of explaining, I walk fast
and faster until the voices die away. Orange-cap mushroom
in a log gone to coarse dust. The ridge trail tips down

toward the promise of a view. More wind, traffic, three-note
birdsong almost in rhythm with my steps. When the trail ends
on a high knob, I follow a deer path downhill, clamber

through deadfalls thinking of falling, dreaming of flight.
When the path dwindles, I find a sitting log above
the dim valley, the noisy invisible road. Men and women

are hard at work while I loiter and wander and pity myself.
The grapevine goes up thirty feet before it touches wood,
and how did that happen? These slips of wild rose and poison ivy

could be grafted into any poem and take good hold and prosper,
green and noxious, not our friends. The world says many things,
most of them sad and hard. The world has lost many things,

and they all will return, but not as what they were.
From here the trail goes to fantasy and nostalgia, nirvana
and Neil Young. The lesson for today duplicates and defies

the one for yesterday. The tourist train clanks up the valley
and the driver blasts the whistle. There is a way home
from anywhere, past the nurse log and the wolf tree,

over the deer droppings fresh and dried, under one deadfall
and through the next. The squaw root and Indian pipe suckle gently
from the beech roots, taking just enough for bloom and seed.

Doorways

Traffic starts at six on Everett Road, heavy trucks gearing down and clunking over the tracks. Last night, the coyotes howled and yipped and barked off to the south. As we nursed the last wine on the front porch, someone said, *They don't give a rip about us, they're greeting each other,* and someone else, *Then why do they frighten me?* and someone else, *I like the sound as long as I'm six feet from the door and the walls are sound.*

In all those bad movies, the zombies or werewolves or birds batter at the windows and doors while the plucky heroes board themselves in desperately, some dying spectacularly before the inevitable survivals. Showing his slides to us, Nelson said, *I love doorways, windows, and ghost towns.* The bare frames opened onto mountains, oceans of sky, dark threads that could have been rivers.

The coyotes came nowhere near us. They did not disturb my rest. Out in the night, they greeted each other wildly, then went quiet. Without fire or clothing, without windows or doors, they went on teaching the young, sniffing for food, curling together at first light to rest in some deep hollow among the distant rumor of the trucks.

Contemplation with Ledges and Moon

What do the hollows in the stone promise?
Where the scratched names stop, the rock mutters

what it meant all along. Here, the grizzled red maple.
There, yellow beech clenched hard to the cliff side,

a tulip tree smooth forty feet up. Edges blur
in the half-light, and the swallows work higher

and higher, and the bats revel, stretching
their thin webs around what they need.

The mind is a rattly gourd, the ego, a black marble.
The soul is very light and large, a cloud of leaves

that froth and fade into the wood thrush's cry.
There is no soul without the shy veery,

the whiny bugs hunting our heat, the gravel
working its way out from sandstone.

The soul is not a language or a cat or a catapult.
It is a net without mesh, a sail knuckling and filling

among fireflies and gauzy leaves, flowing into
every valley, filling every breath and stone, spinning,

keening, rising, dusty heartwood, silken fog.
The broken path through trees made us stumble,

but we found the wide meadow at last
where the great golden moon lifted up

from the well of her sleep and sent down
more borrowed light than we needed

as we cried out and whispered on our way.

IV

Alba in Everett, Ohio

Just beyond the walls on all sides,
the green, astonishing world.
The fat guy peers out,

scratches his belly, searches
for his lost Latin. The only rule
he remembers: no matter

how weary the traffic,
how dry and hot the dawn,
every morning still delivers

the old and new gospel
of leaf, wing, and shadow.
The bee trapped

between screen and pane
has not moved since sundown
and considers how the fine mesh

it clutches organizes everything.
Surely, escape is just one move away.
The concrete plug that seals

the septic tank waits like Excalibur
for the right hand to grasp
its rusty wire and free the waters.

And the dead branch holds
its finest twigs exactly
where the spring buds should be.

From the Screen Porch

Not early, except for me. Hummers buzzed and zoomed;
blue jays chattered. When the demon demanded
that Shiva surrender his wife, the god opened his third eye

and created a bigger demon. *Eat the small demon,* he said,
but after a long chase the small demon begged Shiva
to save him, and he relented. *You made me to devour,*

complained the big demon; *what shall I eat?* And Shiva:
Why not eat yourself? The demon did, from toes to chin,
until he could eat no more. *This is the face of glory,* Shiva said.

I shall set it at the door of the temple. All this glorious
greenery, entrancing and expensive, I wanted to dissolve
into it, but I pulled out the pencil and the student poems

and made earnest inscrutable notations as the coffee cooled.
Just on the other side of the screen, I felt the hummingbird's
dive and the other fleeing in fear. In the high spruce,

the jay jittered, flashed, and swooped. *This face
is the face of glory,* she said. What *do* the birds know?
I scrawled carefully in the margins, and around my words

the white plane of the page slid away, the floor tiles
cooled my feet, the air opened and wandered all directions.
Devour myself? Yes. But why stop? I want to eat the world,

hummers and high pines and jays and deep earth and all,
eat and eat until inside and out sizzle and fuse and the face
of glory shines like a star and the great door opens at last.

Mountain Dawns

1.
Hummingbirds dive and scrap for first chance at the feeder;
scrub jays pose with their round heads and outlaw eyes.

In the high woods, any voice carries for miles:
a father, wheels on pavement, the jet from Denver.

The ones I love sleep. The aspens quiver as if they know
what's coming. If I could name the trees, I might name them

Strong-of-Root, Bends-to-Light, Wind-Catcher.
And the rocks: Hunkers-and-Holds, Sleeps-All-Day.

And here at my right hand, so quiet I nearly missed it,
the beautiful Lake the Size of My Head.

2.
I wake earlier each morning, annoy the others
as I stumble into clothes and out the door.

Gray squirrel carries a scrap away.
The shadow-soft valley reaches west, one bare crest ablaze.

Sometimes I lock all the doors,
and the spiders and ants still walk right in.

At last, sun on my dark shirt
like a blessing.

3.
Every morning I make the coffee stronger,
but the trees and rocks are just as far away.

Fly-hum, wind in leaves, slow tires on gravel.
A few roads and many trails. The birds fly where they please.

One day I'll just quit looking for the path.
In the high woods, a man can walk anywhere under the trees.

It is hard to fly, says the ruby throat. *But I love to be breathless.*
I love to spend all day drinking only what is sweet.

The Music of What Happened

The sweetest music of all
Is the music of what happens.
—Irish folk saying

So after two days drenched, swimming, drowning in music,
I woke early and headed out to run. Nobody on campus

but the geese and crows. I dodged the goose crap and found
Columbia Lake, blue on the map but mainly mud in truth,

a little water threading through. A catbird chased the robins,
a red-winged blackbird muddled in the long grass,

two goldfinches darted away from the dirt track and led me
to the real creek, spring-strong and almost clear.

A pair of willows, grasses, boot prints, and the rush of water
down a rocky riffle. The music of what happens

in a sweet glade not far from the power lines: clamors,
chords, voices loud and sweet and slow, solo and chorus.

This music is not soul or fingers, not breath through brass
or cords of flesh, not mind or heart. It is the whole being,

blood and tendon, neuron and electron, mitochondria
and muscle, darting eye and spinning dream, all tuned

and tuning, turning, dancing, portals, ports in the storm,
gifts offered and accepted, maps and instruments,

instructions and provisions, salt pork and molasses,
barley and cider for the winter, the oil and the lamp

for burning, the cabin in the clearing and the path
that leads home to the music, the music that is the path.

Waterloo, 30 May 2004

Spring Tractates

Past the houses—past the headlands—
Into deep Eternity—
—Emily Dickinson, #76

I.

When it rains, it rains. When it rains and then fades
to a dismal drizzle, I walk to church anyway, clutch the umbrella

and pass under the blooming pear tree and across the street.
When I feel this greedy and restless, I grumble and annoy

my wife even more than usual. I scribble while the choir labors
earnestly through the anthem, may the mind of Christ live in me,

Amen. My pastor says Jesus still walks among us. He says little.
He ate fish with the disciples at Emmaeus, touched their perfect bodies,

lit their minds. Why am I restless when I have a big house,
many rooms, many windows, many doors? Like my preacher,

I was a nervous boy, worried mostly about the wrong things,
which is a kind of comfort now. Yesterday I bought six used books,

bored with all my dreary devices, dreaming of some musty page
that would charge everything again. For three bucks, I got all

the poems of Emily Dickinson—six for each penny. I came home
and read *Exultation is the going / Of an inland soul to sea*. I read

Bred as we, among the mountains, / Can the sailor understand /
The divine intoxication / Of the first league out from land? I'm a long way

from water. Fifty days to Pentecost. Patience, my pastor says.

II.

Absence makes the heart grow fodder.

The toddler on the sidewalk has learned the harmonica's secret—
breathe in, blow out, every note is sweet.

Its second secret rests in the space between the breaths.

I can see so far and touch so little.

For a week after I fell on the bike,
I forgot the scrapes along one shin,
but today I remembered
and flaked off the scabs until one bled.

After two glorious weeks, it was cloudy all day.
Out east, one milk-blue skein where the clouds have loosened.

How many rich browns and tans and grays
in the flaking stump at the water's edge?

Absence makes the heartwood falter.

Ha.

III.

My soul—accused me—And I quailed
As Tongues of Diamond had reviled
All else accused me—and I smiled—
My Soul—that Morning—was my Friend
—#753

Out the front door, ratty Scotch pine, then the parking lot.
Side windows: spiderwebbed blacktop of the driveway,

then the gray neighbor house, A/C unit, pile of old brick
under the seedy stairway to the second floor. In back,

grass and yard violets and dandelions, bird feeders,
no birds this morning. All sunk in green and dismal

domesticity, or so says my diamond-tongued soul.
It trusts nothing in this world, believes stoutly

in this world, rests hard in this world.

IV.

Oh Emily, you found a way out of town
so strange and clever nobody could follow.

How did you do it?
The first league is astonishing,
but the water is wide, the sky is gray,
the compass wanders like a weary drunk.

It's been centuries, or years,
or all day.

Whose road is this?

V.

Ah, admit it, all this angst and melancholy is phony—
these last weeks I've been smug

as a grain-fed trout as the spring unfolded
like God's own fancy parasol.

Even now, real live horses canter down the bike path,
and how can I worry about the gray in my beard

or soaring Chinese oil consumption or even
the misery and rubble my tax dollars are buying

when the cardinals are showing off
and the mallard sprints toward the far shore

with its green head glowing
and all the hard work happening out of sight?

All over town, the lilacs pour out clouds of essence,
and any walk means passing through

a dozen fragrant little heavens.

VI.

High up, the new cottonwood leaves
shine like mirrors,

like the starling's purple helmet.
In this much sun, everything blazes,

even the water shines.
The black snake ripples upstream

as quiet and dark as pure space,
as a man's or a woman's hunger.

VII.

Once I tried to sleep on roots and gravel
high in some foothills,

a cold April and the last firewood
bleeding into ash.

An intricate song washed everything
like a black dry ocean,

and I heard every note
and remembered everyone I had failed and deserted.

And then my soul, or some soul,
curled itself around me

like the down bag I didn't own.
It didn't speak a word, but I listened—

and centuries or years or hours later,
a shape felt its way out of darkness, and another,

and between them I saw four smooth stones,
four steps I could take.

Some Lines for Lincoln, O.

She told them the only grace they could have was the grace they could imagine.
—Toni Morrison, *Beloved*

In the dawn, I half thought the horses were statues—
three full-grown and a colt outside the white stable.
Now it's dusk. The swaybacked dark one nickered as I passed,

then the high valley stilled again, its rough zigzag fences
and tan grasses easing up into the tree line. I'm a stranger
in Lincoln, where all fall the students have been arguing

and reading the great books and God and each other.
They sit now with the same slightly weary ease as the horses,
though they talk a lot more. They say love and God

and black and white more carefully than when they came.
They talk all at once, and then all want to wait their turn;
their most graceful passionate speeches end in questions.

I don't know them, but I love it here already, these horses
and the valley as it goes dark, the black cat who rubs my legs
and jumps up to be petted, purring loudly, wanting both my hands

How much does it cost the clouds to spread so thin along the ridge?
What's lost if I pet the cat instead of writing in my book?
These are not the real questions, just the ones I ask as I wait,

as the pink light deepens along the miles of cloud.
The father said: When you breathe in, say *Thank you.*
When you breathe out, say *Goodbye.* I always forget.

Today we contended on slavery, ghosts, memories
that are not ours. The valley darkens, the black mare
stands in the snow. Tomorrow, Salinger.

“Then in a Wailful Choir the Small Gnats Mourn”

And why so sad and angry
re October
season of mists and
mellow fruitfulness and all

How much there is
to explain and reckon
the mower whose wheels
keep turning
even in their sleep
the cousin still surviving
through a tube

Today I blew free
blasted toward some
old horizon
by winds to which
I cannot help but yield
as the leaves cannot help
but yellow and confess

as the quarry must give
back their image
curled and shaking
in mindless
minor glory

as whatever touches it
the water must accept

Early Walk with Big Willow and Demiurge

Yes, even before eight it was muggy, the underbrush soggy,
the air thick as mucus. Yes, there were the attendant
buzzers and whiners, bloodsuckers all. But there was the sun,

still convinced that today things would go just right.
There was a path behind the upper woodpile that
I hadn't noticed yesterday, an easy walk back to the swamp,

where the biggest deer I've ever seen clumped recklessly away.
There was the big willow at the water's edge, and
beneath its curtain I considered the browning lilies.

There's the channel lined with timbers on one side—thirty yards
and it stops in a tangle of weeds. Whoever made all this,
others have been tinkering ever since. I could believe

like the Gnostics that the big god got too busy
making black holes and regulating nebulae and put
some young helper to this job, not a bad god but perhaps

overconfident. I can see him thinking it was time
for some new ideas, e.g. buzzes, stabs, and whines.
I could believe the new god overlooked some details—

if there has to be humidity, couldn't we *like* it?
But imagine the big god coming by to check it out
and smiling, edgy as a father whose son brings home

the bookshelf he built in shop, all askew, varnish dripping.
Imagine the old god trying to say something nice,
admiring the canyons and mountains and all those

good beasts and trees, then hurrying off to adjust a star
that needed to go nova in nine million years.
It was cool in the cabin, where the A/C ran all night.

Outside a few early leaves made their one big trip,
and the rest sucked at the sunlight. The hummers sipped
at the dirty feeder—nobody has cleaned it all summer,

but we keep filling it up—as if they couldn't believe their luck.

Furnace Run, Sunday

I can barely stand the sound of my boots, so I slow down
and down some more. Fine day, sun and breeze

in the high limbs and birdsong like confetti and one bee.
Without touching a thing, I hear water and traffic behind.

God bless the air. And what do I know? That the creek
is low and smells of fish and liberty. A few names of things,

and some ghosts I brought along: one lanky and owlish,
one kneeling to the next small wonder, one who said,

Are you gonna drop your rock or take it with you?
I believe I know how to get back, where to meet

my friends. The breeze is cool, the sun is warm;
if I wanted, I could wade through the creek to where

the ripe grass heads nod like the elders. Instead
I will sit and sit, and despite my stiff neck and many failings,

I will slip out of myself and sail toward the place
within this place. Black butterfly dancing upstream,

I will be light as you are. I will dance instead of walking.
Red stone that holds me up, I will want only

to wait as long as I must. Silver, yellow, green skin
of water, I will learn to speak what the rocks are hinting.

I will gather all that rises, moves, shines, accept
each light and leaf and creature dipping carefully to drink,

hold them in my warm hands like wine and bread
until we all are served, and then give everything away.

Contemplation at the Bar R Ranch

Both the owner and his daughter said we'd have to see the crosses,
so of course I tried to avoid them. But wandering aimlessly

after sublimity as I do on free afternoons, I followed a sign
that said "Baptismal" down a narrow way

and stepped carefully on rocks across the icy creek.
When I looked up, there they were, enormous,

big enough to crucify a pteranodon or a giraffe.
As I climbed the muddy path, some part of me said,

I have to safeguard my doubts, and another remembered
how the old picker said to Goodman, *I find*

the prettiest woman in the room and play every song for her.
Too edgy to eat, Salinger's Franny tried to pray

the Jesus prayer all the way through homecoming.
With the sun low behind the crosses, I could barely look.

Thin grass, lichens, rocks, and gravel lay low all around,
stunned by some brutal devotion not their own.

Three weeks to solstice. Faint thin birdsong.
So many trees, so many rocks, so many women

whose lives and bodies I will never touch.
The creek rippled on, Shasta glowed in the chilly haze,

a strand of spider silk glinted in and out of sight.
Breathe in: *This is paradise.* Breathe out: *I must go.*

From the Rocks at Dusk

I didn't expect this much light. The heavy earth had spun us away from the moon and the sun, but still the lights on their poles blazed like barren torches and every window leaked, the filaments aglow and the photons slashing everywhere, altering everything, not at all like the bat that darted and swung above us in search of the earliest mosquitos. More like the wail and moan of the highway, each passage singular but homogenized by speed and distance, each minivan and semi reduced to an abstract moan.

I wanted to walk back into the woods, pull them up around me like a hooded sweatshirt, and how vain was that? Every tree has its story, but none of them was testifying, with immunity or without. Nothing is lost, but some things are broken, some are splintered, some must wait longer than fossils for regeneration or a good cool drink.

While my eyes were adjusting, I remembered the difference between desire and need. I recalled just what my will means to the world at large. Then I tried bargaining, and pretending not to care, and blinking and glancing sideways. I would tell you what finally worked, if anything had worked. I have about as much patience as a gnat. There weren't any gnats.

I kept pushing the pen across paper, breathed twice slowly, straightened my back. The wet dirt was still cold with winter, its small lives just stirring. Some odd phrases slipped through me like eels. Water muttered on down the creek, bending to geography, obeying the urge to settle. There were many small lights in the great darkness, and as every one of us fell deeper into evening, I found myself believing that the darkness itself was on fire.

Redwing Pond

Dragonfly dances precise and casual,
returns to the same broken cattail,

dances again among stems
like rusty antennas decorated

with stuffing from the car seats.
Pond leaves like oval coins,

tossed by some spendthrift
to hold up the reddish small blooms.

Here the junkyard and the factory and
the palace of love are only inches apart.

A frog screeches and dives with every step.
The wild rose's new shoots are red as cherries.

The dragonflies mate shamelessly
on the wing, faithless and pure.

What reason for any of this?
The water lily glows in the sun—

a soft moon, a cool candle,
a doorway lit from within.

“Night, the Astonishing . . .”

One star only, and all the trees looming, not my enemies
nor my friends. Hölderlin praises the night: “the stranger

to all that is human,” “mournful and gleaming.”
But this night is wet heat and the insects that crave

any blood the way I crave red wine and whisky,
sweet words in a row, and whatever it is we call God.

Inside, the lights press against the window,
show the stove and shelves, the table with its bottles,

all these homely things shining and the night behind them.
Luna pads to the door, and I let her out. It’s late.

I am not a cat or a soldier to be out in the dark,
not the farmer in his roaring combine, taking off the wheat

before it rains. I walked in the hot woods all day,
I read and hummed and muttered on the soul and the spirit,

but there is no more in me than one star might say:
that it fused and changed itself for centuries, consumed

its own being to cast something outward, that its hot light
sailed reckless as Lucifer through oceans of space

to wash up on this undreamed, dark, occupied island,
to be gathered and known, to be spoken among the trees.

Credits

Many thanks to the editors of these journals, where these poems have appeared (sometimes in different versions):

Adirondack Review: "The Recovery of Imaginary Friends"; *Antioch Review:* "Interior Colloquy in Glen Helen"; *Artful Dodge*: "An Hour"; *Brevity*: "Hum"; *Christian Century*: "Praise Is a Language," "Firefly"; *Colorado Review*: "Damselfly," "Ode to Luna with Implausible Quotations"; *Lake Effect*: "The Song of the Weed Witch"; *Hayden's Ferry Review*: "Rules (Observed and Unwritten) for Hot Sundays in the Heart of the Empire"; *Mid-American Review*: "Soul Travel at the Electric Brew, Goshen, Indiana," "Where Water Finds an Edge"; *The New Pantagruel*: "Advice for Walkers," "Note from the Week after Next," "We Go Out Searching for Sermons in Stone"; *Nimrod:* "Settle"; *North American Review*: "Day at the Pond without Geese"; *Oregon Extension Journal*: "Some Lines for Lincoln, O."; *Pebble Lake Review:* "February Report on Conditions in the Interior"; *Phoebe*: "Letter to Students Gone for Summer"; *Poet Lore*: "Furnace Run, Sunday," "'Then in a Wailful Choir the Small Gnats Mourn'"; *Rampike*: "Astonishing Details of the Universe"; *Rhubarb*: "Letter with melody and Fall From Chair," "Lunch Poem at Snow Road," "Report on Recent Activities in Austin (Selected)"; *River Styx:* "Signature, or Jonathan Edwards and Joe Walsh Meet in the Electric Brew"; *Shenandoah:* "Fulks Run to Cumberland"; *Spoon River Poetry Review*: "The Vice President for Obscure Relations Rises to Offer Something Resembling an Explanation"; *Tampa Review:* "From the Screen Porch"; *Whiskey Island*: "The Poet on the Beaver Marsh," "Futurism in the Black Swamp," "Structural Adjustments to Maintain Growth Will Be Necessary."

"The Music of What Happened" was first published in *Sound In the Land: Essays on Mennonites and Music*, ed. Maureen Epp and Carol Ann Weaver (Kitchener, ON: Pandora Press, 2005).

Many thanks to the Ohio Arts Council, the Antioch Writers' Workshop, the Language of Nature Institute, the Cuyahoga Valley Environmental Education Center, and Susan Carpenter for the loan of the Snow Road cabin. I also owe thanks to my colleagues and students at Bluffton University, who teach me in ways both direct and oblique. Thanks, always, to Marlyce and Nathan, Jessica, Ben, and Joel, marvelous presences. And for counsel, advice, and complaints on these poems and for their ongoing friendship, special thanks to Terry Hermsen, Jean Janzen, Julia Levine, Clint McCown, Kevin Stein, Keith Ratzlaff, and Julia Kasdorf.

This book is dedicated to my first and best teacher, Nick Lindsay.

About the Author

Jeff Gundy has taught at Bluffton University since 1984. He has published four full-length collections of poetry, most recently *Deerflies*, which won the Editions Prize and the Nancy Dasher Award. His three prose books include the award-winning *Walker in the Fog: On Mennonite Writing*. Recipient of several Ohio Arts Council fellowships, Gundy is a 2008 Fulbright Lecturer at the University of Salzburg, Austria.